Presented To:

Presented By:

Date:

from a
Wife's
Heart
to her
Husband

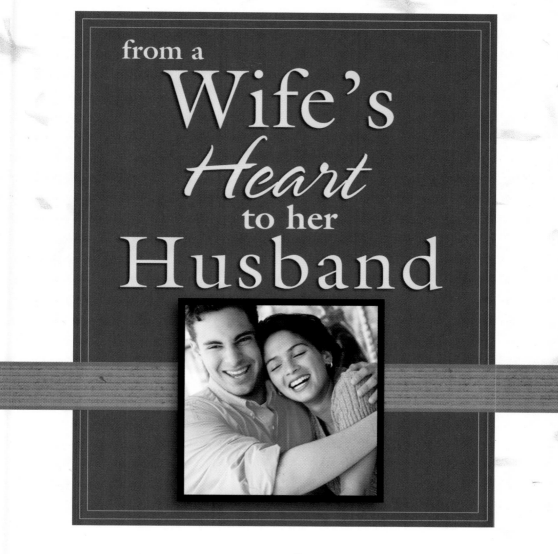

NELSON BOOKS
A Division of Thomas Nelson Publishers
Since 1798

www.thomasnelson.com

Published in Nashville, Tennessee, by Thomas Nelson, Inc.

Nelson Books titles may be purchased in bulk for educational, business, fund-raising, or sales promotional use. For information, please e-mail SpecialMarkets@ThomasNelson.com.

Scripture quotations noted NKJV are from the New King James Version®. Copyright © 1979, 1980, 1982 by Thomas Nelson, Inc. Used by permission. All rights reserved.

Scripture quotations noted AMP are from The Amplified Bible: Old Testament. Copyright © 1962, 1964 by Zondervan Publishing House (used by permission); and from THE AMPLIFIED NEW TESTAMENT. Copyright © 1958 by the Lockman Foundation (used by permission).

Scripture quotations noted CEV are from The Contemporary English Version. © 1991 by the American Bible Society. Used by permission.

Scripture quotations noted MSG are from The Message. Copyright © by Eugene H. Peterson 1993, 1994, 1995. Used by permission of NavPress Publishing Group.

Scripture quotations noted NCV are from The Holy Bible, New Century Version, copyright © 1987, 1988, 1991 by Word Publishing, a division of Thomas Nelson, Inc. All rights reserved. Used by permission.

Scripture quotations noted NIV are from the Holy Bible: New International Version®. Copyright © 1973, 1978, 1984 by International Bible Society. used by permission of Zondervan Publishing House. All rights reserved.

Scripture quotations noted NLT are from the Holy Bible, New Living Translation, copyright © 1996. Used by permission of Tyndale House Publishers, Inc., Wheaton, Illinois 60189. All rights reserved.

Scripture quotations noted NRSV are from the New Revised Standard Version of the Bible. Copyright © 1989 by the Division of Christian Education of the National Council of the Churches of Christ in the U.S.A. All rights reserved.

Managing Editor: Lila Empson
Associate Editor: Kyle L. Olund
Manuscript: Sheila Rabe
Design: Whisner Design Group, Tulsa, Oklahoma

ISBN 0-7852-1479-8

Printed in the United States of America

06 07 08 09 QW 5 4 3 2 1

Love is not something you feel.
It's something you do.

David Wilkerson

Contents

Introduction

You, my dear husband, are one of a kind, a man among men. You are the most important person in the world to me. Your love is my greatest possession. I value your good opinion of me more than anyone else's. Your success makes me happy, and I can't be content unless you are content.

I hope as you read the words in this book you will see my love on every page. Being your wife is a joy for me, and you make traveling life's road an interesting journey. I want you to know that if I had it to do all over again, I'd still choose you over any other man. I also hope as you read this book that you'll realize what an important part you play, not only in my life, but also in the lives of many people. You hold an important spot in the world, a spot reserved specially for you by God.

Spread love everywhere you go: first of all in your own house.

Mother Teresa

Beloved, let us love one another, for love is of God; and everyone who loves is born of God and knows God.

1 John 4:7 NKJV

No hero, real or imagined,
can compare to a good husband.

You are my hero.

Heroes can be found everywhere—running across the big screen in a movie theater, fighting their way through the covers of a history book or novel, even being lauded in the newspaper. For me there is no hero like you, my husband. You are the unsung opener of difficult jars, the fixer of squeaky stairs, and the killer of spiders. You'll leave a warm bed in the middle of the night to investigate because I heard a strange noise. You soldier on at your job just to make sure I am taken care of. You are my protector, lover, and friend, someone I look to in times of trouble. Lois Lane can keep her Superman. You are all I need.

There, under the shadow of a man's strength, a woman finds rest.

John Eldredge

My beloved is all radiant and ruddy,
distinguished among ten thousand.

Song of Solomon 5:10 NRSV

*I may consult with my friends,
but you are my most trusted advisor.*

I appreciate and count on your advice.

I like to talk to my girlfriends about my problems, but when it comes to my deepest needs and my biggest troubles, I turn to you, my other half, my lifetime partner. I know I can count on you to step back from any emotional landslide and look at my problem logically. You provide a fresh pair of eyes and a male perspective. Because you know me best and love me best and want what's best for me, I can trust you to help me sort through my options and make the right decision. You are my team captain, and you always have a game plan. I know you will give me good advice because you want us both to come out as winners.

No gift is more precious than good advice.

Erasmus

The teaching of a wise person gives life.
It is like a fountain that can save people from death.

Proverbs 13:14 NCV

I appreciate it when you do as much to keep me as you did to get me.

Our love grows and our marriage benefits by your continued consideration for me.

Cross the mountain, swim the stream, kill the dragon, let me drive your car. Once upon a time there was nothing you wouldn't do to win me, and that was exciting. What is even more exciting is the fact that now you have me, you're still willing to do whatever it takes to keep me. You're still my greatest admirer and the king of kind gestures. Every time you bring me flowers or ask what I'd like to do for fun, you show me that I'm still special to you. Every woman wants to be treasured, not just when she's young and cute, but all her life. What a wonderful thing it is that you treasure me and that I have your actions as proof.

> Husbands who have the courage to be tender enjoy marriages that mellow through the years.
>
> Brendan Francis

Husbands should love their wives as [being in a sense] their own bodies. He who loves his own wife loves himself. For no man ever hated his own flesh, but nourishes and carefully protects and cherishes it, as Christ does the church.

Ephesians 5:28–29 AMP

We are a team, so the best way out of any difficult situation is together.

If we always remember that we are a team no matter what, our relationship will be good no matter what.

Hard times have a way of dividing and conquering a couple, confusing them and spinning them around with blame and accusation until they lose sight of the real problem. Pretty soon instead of attacking the problem they're attacking each other. I never want to fight against you. I want to be on your side and fight with you. When hard times hit, I want to stand next to you and help hit back. I know you want to do the same for me. Let's always remember that God put us together and that together we're twice as strong. When bad things happen, let's never turn on each other, but turn back to back and fight them together.

> Alone we can do so little; together we can do so much.
>
> Helen Keller

Two are better than one, because they have a good reward for their toil. For if they fall, one will lift up the other; but woe to one who is alone and falls and does not have another to help.

Ecclesiastes 4:9–10 NRSV

You can say anything to me as long as you say it in love.

Your consideration for my feelings will help me face hard truths and make it easier for us to work through difficult issues.

I enjoy it when you say nice things to me. I feast on every compliment. Much as I love those sweet words, I know there will be times when you must tell me hard truths. My friends may not always want to point out my missteps or potential problems, but because you love me like only a husband can, I know you will. When you have to tell me painful truths, I hope you'll always ease the sting with a good dose of love. Give it to me straight, but give it to me kindly. Don't hold anything back, but remember to hold me. When you have to say something I won't want to hear, I promise to listen. But I'll hear best if you say it gently.

The kindest word in all the world is the unkind word unsaid.

Author Unknown

Speaking the truth in love, we will in all things grow up into him who is the Head, that is, Christ.

Ephesians 4:15 NIV

Because you follow God I can trust you to lead us safely.

As long as you trust God to guide your decisions, your decisions will always be wise ones.

Some husbands simply can't be trusted. They use poor judgment, make bad decisions, and make their wives nervous and worried. They follow their impulses and trust their own wisdom to guide them. But you look to wisdom greater than your own. You look to God to guide your decision-making, and you allow His rules to govern your behavior. That is why I trust you. I trust you with my heart because I know you would never intentionally break it. I trust you with our finances because I know you won't act selfishly. Because you want to live a life that makes God happy, you live in a way that makes me happy too. Your wise leadership contributes to my good night's sleep every night.

Wisdom is the ability to use knowledge so as to meet successfully the emergencies of life. Men may acquire knowledge, but wisdom is a gift direct from God.

Bob Jones

Only the Lord gives wisdom; he gives knowledge and understanding.

Proverbs 2:6 NCV

No hero, real or imagined, can compare
to a good husband.

You can say anything to me as long as
you say it in love.

Because you follow God I can trust
you to lead us safely.

*Admitting your mistakes
makes you a big man.*

*Being brave enough to admit your mistakes
makes you a big man, especially in my eyes.*

It can be hard to admit when you're wrong. It's not a guy kind of thing to do. A man maintains respect by never backing down, never backing off, and never stopping to ask for directions. Right? To admit you were wrong is to acknowledge weakness. But to admit you were wrong is also to admit the truth. That's vital, because wrong things need to be fixed and it's hard to fix what you don't acknowledge—rather like standing on the deck of the *Titanic* saying, "What iceberg?" When you admit your mistakes, others appreciate your honesty. They think, "Here's a man who's not afraid to be human. I can trust him to deal straight with me." The confidence your humility inspires in others is what makes you a big man.

> More people would learn from their mistakes if they weren't so busy denying them.
>
> Harold J. Smith

Confess to one another therefore your faults (your slips, your false steps, your offenses, your sins) and pray [also] for one another, that you may be healed and restored [to a spiritual tone of mind and heart]. The earnest (heartfelt, continued) prayer of a righteous man makes tremendous power available [dynamic in its working].

James 5:16 AMP

*Your true success stretches beyond
the borders of the workplace.*

*Always look at the big picture of your life,
and you'll see how really successful you are.*

I look at you and see a man smart enough to avoid confining the measure of his success to the workplace. That is only a small part of who you are. You want to achieve in all areas of your life, mastering new skills and meeting new challenges. You want to be rich in good relationships. You want to pursue hobbies and interests that develop new strengths and talents. Please don't limit your definition of success to promotions and raises, because who you are is so much bigger than what you do at work. I hope you'll always keep your life rich in interests, in working with good causes, and investing in the people who are important to you. That is the mark of a truly successful man.

A man can be so busy making a living that he forgets to make a life.

William Barclay

One man considers himself rich, yet has nothing [to keep permanently]; another man considers himself poor, yet has great [and indestructible] riches.

Proverbs 13:7 AMP

The way to your wife's heart is through her honey-do list.

Help me tackle those difficult household tasks, and I-love-you's will come through loud and clear.

Flowers are great, dinner out is a nice treat, and compliments are much appreciated. And, in case you've forgotten, chocolate is always a tasteful offering. But when you get to the honey-do list, you really get me. That's because the items on that list aren't usually wife-friendly chores. Fix the leak under the sink— sprawl under there at an awkward angle and get dripped on? Not likely. Change the oil in the car— yuck! There are just some household chores better matched to a man's genes than a woman's. When you do those things for me it makes my life so much easier. And when you use your valuable time to do them, it spells *LOVE* in capital letters.

> Love is not something you feel. It's something you do.
>
> David Wilkerson

Each of you should look not only to your own interests,
but also to the interests of others.

Philippians 2:4 NIV

Your generosity proves how confident and capable you are.

Your generous attitude makes me proud.

When you're generous it says many things to me. It speaks of your kind heart and your willingness to reflect the generous nature of God. It also says something that you might not be aware of. It testifies that you are a man who can afford to be generous because you're capable of replacing whatever you give away. You're confident that your strength and ability, guided by the hand of God, will bring in whatever we need, so you are happy to share with others who may be less capable. I hope you never listen when fear tempts you to turn miserly. Remain confident in God's power and your abilities. Keep an open hand. Stay generous. There's no need to be anything less.

The world says, The more you take, the more you have. Christ says, The more you give, the more you are.

Frederick Buechner

Those who are generous are blessed,
for they share their bread with the poor.

Proverbs 22:9 NRSV

*Good friends and interesting hobbies
are as important as a 401(k) plan.*

*The friendships you're developing and
the activities you're enjoying will benefit
you both now and in the future.*

Every man eventually reaches retirement if he lives long enough. Most men plan for it in varying degrees, depending on pension plans or investments to carry them through their post-work years. But not all men consider the other investments they need to ensure a good retirement. Because you're a wise man, I know when you look ahead you see the big picture. You understand it takes more than money to make those golden years golden. You know you'll need a reason to get up in the morning and buddies to encourage you to keep going and doing in spite of the aches and pains of old age. Go out with the guys with my blessing. Pursue your interests, and develop your support system. I understand that you're investing in your future.

> The better part of one's life consists of his friendships.
>
> Abraham Lincoln

A friend loves you all the time, and a brother helps in time of trouble.

Proverbs 17:17 NCV

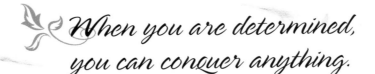

When you are determined, you can conquer anything.

Keeping your eyes fixed on your goals and remaining determined not to give up will help you meet and master any challenge.

The most powerful tool you own is the manly determination God put in you, that driving power that kicks in when you face a challenge or problem. It's what makes you clench your jaw and roll up your sleeves and mutter, "I will not be beaten by this." It's what turns your brain to problem-solving instead of worrying. It's what makes you proactive rather than reactive. It will give you courage to face discouragement and naysayers. It will give you the strength to push past obstacles and make good things happen. Some men tend to neglect this tool; they let it sit around and get rusty. But I'm confident you won't do that. Whatever challenges you may face, your determination will carry you through.

Let us not be content to wait and see what will happen, but give us the determination to make the right things happen.

Peter Marshall

Do you not know that those who run in a race all run, but one receives the prize? Run in such a way that you may obtain it.

1 Corinthians 9:24 NKJV

Your true success stretches beyond the borders of the workplace.

Good friends and interesting hobbies are as important as a 401(k) plan.

Your generosity proves how confident and capable you are.

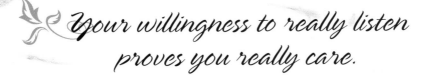

*Your willingness to really listen
proves you really care.*

*Your willingness to listen inspires
me to share with you my deepest
thoughts and concerns.*

Women love to talk. You probably figured that out long ago. We talk when we're happy, we talk when we're excited, and we really like to talk when we have a problem. Talking helps us cope with our troubles, disappointments, and frustrations. Some men can turn all that talking into background noise and tune it out. Thanks for not doing that. Thanks for showing genuine interest in my thoughts and concerns, for reining in your frustration when you don't agree with what I'm saying and instead patiently listening. When you listen it speaks volumes to me. It says you care about what I feel and think. It tells me I'm important to you and that what I have to say matters. Thanks for being a good listener.

> One of the best ways to demon-strate God's love is to listen to people.
>
> Bruce Larsen

My dear brothers and sisters, always be willing to listen and slow to speak. Do not become angry easily.

James 1:19 NCV

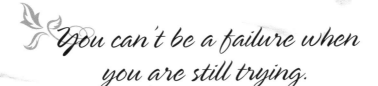
*You can't be a failure when
you are still trying.*

*Never see yourself as a failure because
God doesn't, and neither do I.*

It's easy for some husbands to let discouragement tarnish their self-image, to look in the mirror and see a failure. But there is a big difference between failing and being a failure. Failure in itself is a mark of courage, because if you fail at something that means you have at least tried, and trying is the trademark of a successful man. True failure lies in never trying, because to not try is to lack courage and faith in God's guidance. The fact that you get up every morning and face a new day of challenges says that you're still in the game. So I hope, even when things aren't going according to plan, that you'll never look in the mirror and see a failure, because you're not.

> The greatest failure is the failure to try.
>
> William Arthur Ward

No matter how many times you trip them up, God-loyal people don't stay down long. Soon they're up on their feet, while the wicked end up flat on their faces.

Proverbs 24:16 MSG

Sometimes it's better to look at life with a child's-eye view.

By keeping alive those good childhood attitudes, you make each day of our life together special.

Adulthood can be great. (Just ask any child who wants to be one!) Grownups drive cars, stay up late, and don't have to eat their vegetables. Of course, we also have to work and shoulder responsibilities that were not part of childhood. Sometimes those important responsibilities of adulthood make us lose track of the innocence and joy we had as children. I hope you'll always value those childlike traits that some adults scorn. I hope you'll choose trust in both God and others over cynicism, that you'll take time to laugh, and that you'll never lose the ability to be easily pleased by the simple things that make everyday living so sweet. I love you and appreciate your maturity, but always keep the child in you alive. I like him, too.

> Seek the wisdom of the ages but look at the world through the eyes of a child.
>
> Ron Wile

I tell you the truth, anyone who will not receive the kingdom of God like a little child will never enter it.

Mark 10:15 NIV

Compliment my cooking and I guarantee you will always eat well.

A sincere compliment when you've enjoyed a meal is always in good taste.

Creating in the kitchen is an art form. Putting together ingredients, combining tastes and textures, ensuring a good nutritional balance—it all takes thought, preparation, time, and labor. It's a labor of love, and you are well worth the effort. I'll make even more of an effort if I know I'm cooking for my biggest culinary fan. So dish out the compliments. Smile and show me you love my cooking and my company. Unlike other artists, my creations don't last, but your appreciation will help the satisfaction of accomplishment linger. If you like something, let me know. When you can see I've outdone myself, state the obvious. I don't mind. Your appreciation is my best inspiration. The more appreciation you show, the more inspired I'll get!

A cheerful look makes a dish a feast.

George Herbert

She's up before dawn, preparing breakfast for her family and organizing her day.

Proverbs 31:15 MSG

My favorite place to sit in church is next to you.

Your presence with me in church reinforces right priorities for us as a couple.

Most people have a favorite spot to sit in church: toward the front where they can see, at the back where they can slip out if they have to leave early, off to the side where their friends sit. But I don't care where I sit as long as it's with you. Being in church together honoring God brings me deep contentment. When we share weekly in that most important experience, it sets our priorities and seals our relationship afresh. There is probably no more lonely experience for a wife than to sit in church without her husband, to participate without the person who is her other half. Thank you for sparing me from that. Thank you for being with me in the place that's best for both of us.

> Church attendance is as vital to a disciple as a transfusion of rich, healthy blood to a sick man.
>
> Dwight L. Moody

Let us not neglect our meeting together, as some people do, but encourage and warn each other, especially now that the day of his coming is drawing near.

Hebrews 10:25 NLT

No matter how you play the game, you are a winner in my eyes.

Win or lose, I'll always think you are fantastic and be proud of you.

On the court or the field, I love watching you in action. As far as I'm concerned, no other guy is worth watching but you. When you're playing games that are more sedentary, I admire your cleverness. In short, I just enjoy seeing you enjoy yourself. Don't ever think you always need to come out a winner for me to admire you. Whether you win or lose is irrelevant to me. I simply like to see you using those manly muscles God gave you. I just want to have fun with you. I don't need a game score to prove to me what I already know: that you're great. I hope you'll remember to enjoy the pleasures God brings your way and forget about who won and who lost.

> Competition is the spice of sports; but if you make spice the whole meal you'll be sick.
>
> George Leonard

You show me the path of life. In your presence there is fullness of joy; in your right hand are pleasures forevermore.

Psalm 16:11 NRSV

Compliment my cooking and I guarantee you will always eat well.

The way to your wife's heart is through her honey-do list.

Your willingness to really listen proves you really care.

*The more you show me you love me
the more love I'll reflect back.*

*Show me loving kindness, and you'll
see it coming right back at you.*

What do a wife and a mirror have in common? Both have a way of reflecting your emotions and actions. Your loving touch encourages me to reach out. Your smile pulls an answering smile from me. Your desire to watch out and care for me inspires me to do the same for you. And those kind gestures— getting me little gifts, running out for ice cream when I've got a craving, fetching a blanket when I'm cold— they make me grateful. They make me want to give back, even outdo you. Your acts of kindness and consideration generate more love between us and allow us both to reflect God's love for us. Keep putting the feeling into action, and we'll continue to raise our relationship to new, exciting heights.

> Spread love everywhere you go: first of all in your own house.
>
> Mother Teresa

Beloved, let us love one another, for love is of God; and everyone who loves is born of God and knows God.

1 John 4:7 NKJV

The happiest home is one where worry is never welcome.

If we focus on trusting God and encouraging each other, we will each benefit, and so will our marriage.

Nothing good can be said about worry. It's an ugly customer that creates misery and havoc wherever it lodges. Worry has no bed-time; it will happily keep you up till all hours; it's never satisfied with simply robbing you of sleep. It steals your joy and undermines your trust in God. It enjoys chipping away at good health and good relationships. It extends unhappiness and shortens tempers. Let's not allow worry to be a guest in our home. When it knocks at our door, let's direct it on to God. That way we'll be free to problem-solve, to focus on the good things in our life and what we have together. Let's keep our home happy by not letting worry in the door.

Oh, how great a peace and quiet-ness would he possess who would cut off all vain anxiety and place all his con-fidence in God.

Thomas à Kempis

Cast all your anxiety on him because he cares for you.

1 Peter 5:7 NIV

The fact that you ignore me when I say "Oh, don't buy me anything" proves you're a genius.

I love getting gifts from you because they are visible proofs of your love.

You are such a smart man! You have figured out that female-speak has a text and a subtext. When I tell you I don't need you to buy me anything, you know that is, of course, not what I'm really saying. What I'm *really* saying is, "I'd feel guilty if you bought me something because you thought you had to, and I don't want you to feel coerced. But I love presents, and I especially love presents from you. I hope you'll go out and do exactly what I asked you not to, because I'll be delighted and flattered if you do." So, why don't I just come out and say that? Different wiring, of course. And, I figure you should know. And you do. Thanks for speaking my language.

> God has given us two hands, one to receive with and the other to give with.
>
> Billy Graham

He brought out gifts of silver and gold and clothing and gave them to Rebekah. He also gave expensive gifts to her brother and mother.

Genesis 24:53 MSG

My love notes from you are treasures I will hoard my whole life.

No love note you write to me will ever be taken for granted.

I enjoy my knickknacks: mementos from our travels, pretty decorations bought on sale, gifts from friends. I love the jewelry you've given me, especially my wedding ring. Our photo albums are equally priceless. The best treasure I'll ever possess, however, is a love note from you, the most important person in my life. I read your tender words and delight in your desire. I smile and think of happy times and shared laughter. Words are important to us women, and yours are important to me, especially the ones you surprise me with on paper. Those words are written proof of what we have. When I hold a love letter from you, I hold the deed to something more valuable than the world's richest gold mine.

When expressions of love are unsolicited, they are invaluable.

Diana Hagee

Many waters cannot quench love, neither can floods drown it. If one offered for love all the wealth of one's house, it would be utterly scorned.

Song of Solomon 8:7 NRSV

Because you understand the importance of teamwork, you value your wife's advice.

Listening to my advice doesn't make you less of a man; it makes you more of a husband.

Teamwork. On the football field, teamwork is what scores the point. In the workplace, teamwork is what gets the project done. And we both know how important teamwork is to a successful marriage. I appreciate the fact that you realize we are a team, each bringing our own unique talents and insights. I'm glad you value my opinions and that you're willing to listen to my advice. It shows how secure you are in your manhood that you can consider another opinion, another way of looking at the world or dealing with a situation. Thank you for not putting me down or shutting me up, for realizing that God gave me to you to help you. Thanks for working as a team. We make a winning combination.

> Who is the wise man? He who learns from all men.
>
> William Gladstone.

The way of a fool is right in his eyes, but he who heeds counsel is wise.

Proverbs 12:15 NKJV

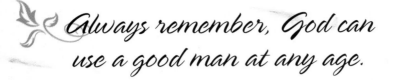

Always remember, God can use a good man at any age.

Always keep your eyes and ears open because God will never stop calling you to new things.

God is always looking for a good man— a man whose heart is willing and whose favorite words are *Yes, Lord*. Some men think God's workforce has an age limit. Isn't it great that they are wrong? God has used all kinds of men throughout history: young and old, weak and strong. That means that at every point in your life you will find God has something for you to do. You'll never have to feel useless or "over the hill" because He will always have a new mountaintop waiting for you. God will never give up using you, no matter what your physical condition or energy level. You will always be valuable and useful to Him.

You are never too old to set another goal or to dream a new dream.

C. S. Lewis

GOD told Abram: "Leave your country, your family, and your father's home for a land that I will show you." So Abram left just as GOD said, and Lot left with him. Abram was seventy-five years old when he left Haran.

Genesis 12:1, 4 MSG

The fact that you ignore me when I say
"Oh, don't buy me anything" proves
you're a genius.

The more you show me you love me the
more love I'll reflect back.

My love notes from you are treasures I
will hoard my whole life.

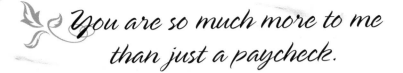 *You are so much more to me than just a paycheck.*

I can always find money somewhere, but I can never find another you.

Some men think their wives see them as only a paycheck. They think, all she wants is to spend my money, all she cares about is how soon I'm going to make more. She wouldn't care if I disappeared tomorrow as long as the money kept coming in. You can rest assured your wife is not that way. I married you, not your income. I married you for your great smile and your kind heart. I married you for the pleasure of your company, not the pleasure of your checkbook. I appreciate how hard you work for us, and I'm happy when we can pay the bills, but this marriage is built on love, not money. Spending your money will never be as important as spending time with you.

> There is no more lovely, friendly, and charming relationship, communion, or company than a good marriage.
>
> Martin Luther

I belong to my lover, and he desires only me.

Song of Solomon 7:10 NCV

*When you use your God-given
talents, you make me proud.*

*I want the best for you, which is
why I want to see you live up to
your full potential.*

God certainly designed someone special
when He made you. With your unique gifts,
you are a man meant to be a useful tool in His
hands. As your biggest fan, I'm all in favor of
that. I appreciate the talents you have, and I
love to see you grow and use them. It makes
me happy when you succeed. I'm as proud of
your accomplishments as you are. I love to see
others benefit from the good fallout that
comes from your usefulness. When I see you in
action, using your mind and your skills, I can't
be anything but proud, because there is nothing better you can do than honor God by
using the gifts God has given you.

> Do what you
> can, with what
> you have, where
> you are.
>
> Theodore Roosevelt

That special gift of ministry you were given when the
leaders of the church laid hands on you and
prayed— keep that dusted off and in use.

1 Timothy 4:14 MSG

It is a mark of wisdom when you can discern the difference between teasing and hurting.

Thank you for remembering that no joke is worth the laugh if it comes at the expense of your wife's feelings.

Some men have tongues sharper than a new saw blade, but their perception is dull as an old axe. With misplaced jests they can cut another person's self-esteem deeply, only to excuse the damage by saying, "Hey, I was only kidding." A laugh at another person's expense really isn't funny, especially to the person who just paid the price for it. Sometimes it can be hurtful and humiliating. That's why I so appreciate the fact that you consider my feelings before speaking. You know my most vulnerable areas and avoid them. You understand that teasing pokes fun at harmless little foibles even I can laugh at, but hurting crosses the line into discomfort. Thank you for knowing where the line is and for keeping a loving distance from it.

> God has set a double fence before the tongue, the teeth and the lips, to teach us to be wary that we offend not with our tongue.
>
> Thomas Watson

Likewise the tongue is a small part of the body, but it makes great boasts. Consider what a great forest is set on fire by a small spark.

James 3:5 NIV

*Your wife is made to share trouble
as well as happiness.*

*God put me by your side so that you don't
have to stand up to hard things alone.*

Who started the rumor that men have to carry burdens alone, that they must be the strong, silent type, going through life with their jaws clenched like Gary Cooper in *High Noon*? Whoever it was, he was wrong. If man was meant to struggle alone, I'm sure there would have been no Eve for Adam. Sorrow is unavoidable, and trouble is part of the package here on earth. But pain can be lifted and troubles more easily overcome by two. Please don't feel that you must keep your concerns bottled up or carry heavy responsibilities single-handed. I'm happy to be your sounding board. I'm your wife, for better or for worse, and I'll be by your side to help in good times and in bad.

Shared joy is double joy, and shared sorrow is half-sorrow.

Swedish Proverb

By helping each other with your troubles,
you truly obey the law of Christ.

Galatians 6:2 NCV

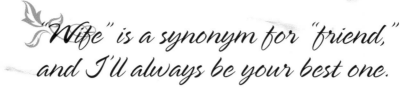 "Wife" is a synonym for "friend," and I'll always be your best one.

Other friends may come and go, but my commitment to you is for a lifetime.

At different stages of our life together, you probably interchange the word *wife* with any number of other words: *lover, partner, household manager, money-spending expert*. But the one word I hope you'll always think of when you think of me is *friend*, because that is what I truly am and will always be. You can tell anything to a friend, which is why I'm always here to listen. You share fun and laughter with a friend, which is why I'm always ready to spend time with you. As true friends, we write our own unique history and forge a loyalty born of commitment. Friends come in all shapes and sizes, and I'm glad you have more than one. But I hope I'll always be your best friend.

Love is rarer than genius itself, and friendship is rarer than love.

Charles Péguy

A friend loves at all times, and kinsfolk are born to share adversity.

Proverbs 17:17 NRSV

To have a happy home is to remember
that God lives in every room.

The best way we can be happy
together is to keep God at the center
of our life together.

I hope home will always be the one place we want to be— a place of contentment, safety, laughter, and smiles, both our refuge and the place where we make some of our happiest memories. We'll always be able to make that possible if we always remember who lives with us. The same God before whom we took our vows lingers with us over morning coffee, encouraging us to share our hearts. He encourages us to settle tiffs and misunderstandings before we go to bed, so that the worst thing we fight over is the covers. When we set goals, He wants us to consider and honor Him. Let's be conscious of God's presence in our home and make it one where He'll feel like one of the family.

> Successful marriage is always a triangle: a man, a woman, and God.
>
> Cecil Meyers

Without the help of the LORD it is useless to build a home or to guard a city.

Psalm 127:1 CEV

You show me you love me by considering my feelings when we're making important decisions.

When you make it your goal that all our major decisions be made in unity, you give me tangible proof of your love.

Nothing is worse for a wife than to feel that her happiness doesn't mater to her husband. When her concerns are dismissed andhen her needs are ignored, words of love ring hollow, and even the most tender touch feels like a joke. Thank you for understanding that. Your willingness to listen to my point of view when we're making decisions shows me you respect me. Your openness to making plans we can both be excited about assures me that I'm part of the team. Your refusal to indulge yourself at the cost of my peace of mind makes me feel more loved than any present you could ever buy me. Your consideration, my darling husband, is all I ever really need.

The vital C's in marriage: Communication, Consideration, Cooperation, Companionship, and Commitment.

Author Unknown

You husbands must give honor to your wives. Treat her with understanding as you live together. She may be weaker than you are, but she is your equal partner in God's gift of new life. If you don't treat her as you should, your prayers will not be heard.

1 Peter 3:7 NLT

*Your wife is made to share trouble
as well as happiness.*

*You are so much more to me than
just a paycheck.*

*When you use your God-given
talents, you make me proud.*

*Turning your dreams into goals
can turn them into reality.*

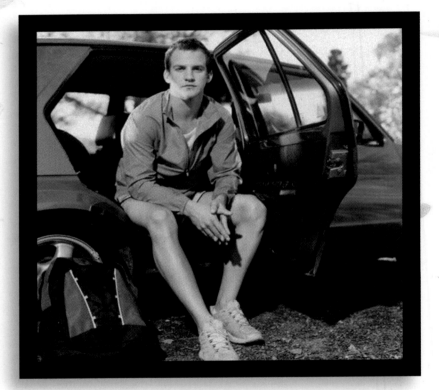

*I'm behind you 100 percent, so take your
dreams to the next level and set the goals
you'll need to meet to make them a reality.*

To have a dream is to acknowledge that God has plans for you. A dream is a gift born of creativity and ambition. The only thing better is a dream come true. Often all that is lacking to make that happen is a goal. A goal makes it all so much more real, doesn't it? It's like being on a football field, keeping your eye on that goal post, and ticking off the yardage you score with each new down. I want to see you make as many of your dreams come true as possible, so I hope you'll boldly set goals and develop a game plan. I know every time you start planning that exciting things will start happening for you.

> A good archer is not known by his arrows but his aim.
>
> Thomas Fuller

I press on toward the goal for the prize of the heavenly call of God in Christ Jesus.

Philippians 3:14 NRSV

Your being a patient husband makes you a dream husband.

Your patience with my faults makes me feel loved, secure, and happy.

Those times that I'm running late when you're ready to go, the shopping expeditions where you wind up waiting in a chair while I make multiple trips between the clothes rack and the dressing room, those reality check moments when we're discussing the health of our check-book— those are the times when your patience makes you as close to perfect as any man can get. I so appreciate your patience. It keeps stress at bay when we're trying to get somewhere. It gives me freedom to take time over my shopping decisions. Most of all, your patience tells me that my needs matter, that I matter. Thank you for fighting off frustration when our differences are driving you crazy, and for remaining calm and considerate. Thanks for being my dream man.

> He who possesses patience possesses himself.
>
> Raymond Lull

Be completely humble and gentle; be patient, bearing with one another in love.

Ephesians 4:2 NIV

You are more than you realize you are.

*God has wonderful things planned
to do in and through you, so never
sell yourself short.*

Life can be a tough opponent with a seemingly endless supply of strategies for taking out your confidence. It likes to try to snatch victory from your hands just when you're feeling like a winner. It tries hard to blind you to opportunities and to block progress. It often dresses up simple detours to look like the end of the road. Life can even try to make you feel like you're nothing. And you know that's wrong because you are something. Don't ever let unimportant details or anyone's false perceptions cloud your vision. You are special. You are made in the image of God. See yourself as God sees you, as I see you— a man of value, here for a purpose.

How you view yourself will determine how far you will go in life.

Author Unknown

God created man in His own image; in the image of God He created him; male and female He created them.

Genesis 1:27 NKJV

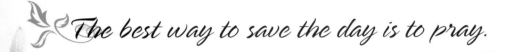

The best way to save the day is to pray.

*Prayer is the most powerful
problem-solving tool we possess.*

We don't need to panic when things don't go right. We don't need to turn ourselves inside out trying to come up with a solution when a problem seems insurmountable. And we don't need to look for a big, red S to plaster on your chest. The first step to solving our problems and the best way to calm our fears is to pray. Prayer plugs us into the greatest power in the universe. Prayer opens our minds to the wisdom of the ages. Prayer takes our focus off our problems and puts it where it needs to be—on God, our protector and provider. Let's remember, my husband, never to panic when trouble comes. Let's remember we can always go to God for help.

> Prayer has a mighty power to sustain the soul in every season of its distress and sorrow.
>
> C. H. Spurgeon

Keep on praying.

1 Thessalonians 5:17 NLT

*You don't have to die to lay down
your life for your wife.*

*Dying to your own wants to care
for my needs is the noblest thing you
can do for me.*

I know you would die for me. If bullets were flying, you'd be my shield. If we were on a sinking ship, you'd give me your spot in the lifeboat. Even without those dramatic opportunities to show your love, you still lay down your life for me more often than you realize. You do it when you give up a Sunday afternoon ballgame on TV in favor of a family outing. You do it when we buy my dream car instead of yours. You do it when you give up that bonus you had plans for to pay a bill. All those decisions where you set aside your own preferences to make me happy make for a noble death that can't go unacknowledged. Thank you, dear husband.

The most satisfying thing in life is to have been able to give a larger part of oneself to others.

Pierre Teilhard de Chardin

Husbands, go all out in your love for your wives, exactly as Christ did for the church— a love marked by giving, not getting.

Ephesians 5:25 MSG

The most important goal you can have is to achieve God's goals for you.

When you make pleasing God your number one priority in life, you're bound to have the best possible life.

Because you love God I know you'll take the important habit of goal-setting one step farther than the average guy and make it your chief aim to achieve God's goals for your life. Any man can set a goal to be a high achiever with an impressive list of accomplishments. But how much better to achieve the great things God has planned for you? Any man can determine to be rich. But how much more excellent to set goals for using those resources wisely! Talents, time, money— when God is at the center of all that goal-setting, you'll really go places. To follow His plan for your life is the best life strategy, and to do what He directs will be your ultimate achievement.

> Never undertake anything for which you would not have the courage to ask the blessing of heaven.
>
> Georg Christoph Lichtenberg

In all your ways know, recognize and acknowledge Him, and He will direct and make straight and plain your paths.

Proverbs 3:6 AMP

You are more than you realize you are.

The most important goal you can have is to achieve God's goals for you.

Turning your dreams into goals can turn them into reality.

Our marriage benefits as much from what you don't buy as from what you do buy.

By resisting purchases we can't afford, we'll do good things for both our budget and our relationship.

Important purchases make our life together secure and comfortable—housing, transportation, investments. Funny though, isn't it, how much we can also benefit by the things we don't buy. Many men yearn for expensive toys that can drain a bank account faster than you can say "Maybe we shouldn't . . ." I appreciate you understanding that money spent impulsively on things that depreciate quickly is irrecoverable. Once it's gone and the garage is full of stuff, there's no replacing it. And there's no avoiding the tagalongs that come with recreational spending: worry, overwork, resentment, quarrels. What a good thing it is for your wife's peace of mind when we steer clear of purchases that will cost us a large amount of misery in exchange for a small amount of pleasure!

Stay out of debt.

Larry Burkett

Let love be your only debt! If you love others,
you have done all that the Law demands.

Romans 13:8 CEV

*Your good character inspires both
my admiration and my trust.*

*Remain an honorable man,
and you'll retain my admiration.*

It's not always easy to be a man of good character. It can cost you business. People may take advantage of you. You may find yourself having to take stands that make you unpopular. It could cost you to be the man you are, but I can assure you of one thing it won't cost you: my respect. I respect you because you have principles you won't sell for money and values you won't trade for friendship, acceptance, or a moment's pleasure. Because of that, I can trust you with my heart. I can trust you to make wise decisions and act in a way that won't hurt us. You have many qualities I appreciate, but the one I admire most is your good character.

A man's reaction to his appetites and impulses when they are roused gives the measure of that man's character.

David McKay

And we, who with unveiled faces all reflect the Lord's glory, are being transformed into his likeness with ever-increasing glory, which comes from the Lord, who is the Spirit.

2 Corinthians 3:18 NIV

God blesses you because you care about proving you're God's gift to only one woman.

Always remember, God made you especially for one woman: me.

Thank you for being a lady's man instead of a ladies' man, for making me the one woman you love to impress. Thank you for concentrating all your love and energy on me, your wife. That kind of commitment earns rewards that a straying husband forfeits. You enjoy a peaceful home, free of tearful scenes and high-voltage wifely wrath. You sleep the restful sleep that comes with a clear conscience. You retain the respect of family and friends. Even more important, you retain your self-respect. You can face yourself in the mirror every morning. Only an insecure man needs to prove he's God's gift to women. You are a special man and a wonderful husband. Trust me. You don't have to prove anything.

> Marriage is not a metaphysical status, which cannot be destroyed; it is rather a moral commitment, which should be honored.
>
> David Atkinson

Let your fountain [of human life] be blessed [with the rewards of fidelity], and rejoice with the wife of your youth. Let her be as the loving hind and pleasant doe [tender, gentle, attractive]; let her bosom satisfy you at all times; and always be transported with delight in her love.

Proverbs 5:18–19 AMP

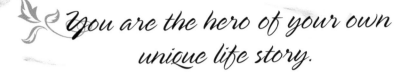

You are the hero of your own unique life story.

Whether they're big or small, you rise to every challenge, and that makes you a hero.

As a little boy you probably pictured yourself as the hero of many an imaginary adventure. You commanded countless battalions of soldiers, carried beautiful women from burning buildings, and saved earth from invading space aliens. You're still a hero, you know. No space aliens to deal with, of course, but now you're fighting for real things, like the security and happiness of your loved ones. When you're not working to provide for us, you're doing battle with leaking pipes, outdoor Christmas lights, and dead car batteries. Neighbors and friends turn to you when they need help. Your every dream, your every talent, the people you impact on a daily basis— they're all part of the unique story of you. You're still a hero.

Faith is the great motive power, and no man realizes his full possibilities unless he has the deep conviction that life is eternally important, and that his work, well done, is part of an unending plan.

Calvin Coolidge

"For I know the plans I have for you," says the LORD, "plans to prosper you and not to harm you, plans to give you hope and future."

Jeremiah 29:11 NIV

*Adversity is the weight training
God uses to strengthen you.*

*Never fear adversity, because
God will bring you through it a
stronger and better man.*

Muscle, the only way you make it bigger is to first tear it down. You get mental and emotional strength the same way, don't you? Funny, isn't it? A man doesn't really grow unless he has to push against difficult circumstances. Mental toughness is hard to develop with no challenges to sharpen your brain. Endurance isn't endurance until it's tested. And determination is only big talk without a problem to prove it. God knows your strengths. He knows your capabilities. He knows how much you can endure and how strong you can become. He will never take you past your limits, but He'll certainly take you to them. And if you can continue to trust Him through the process you'll come out even stronger than you are now.

We are always in the forge, or on the anvil; by trials God is shaping us for higher things.

H. W. Beecher

Consider it wholly joyful, my brethren, whenever you are enveloped in or encounter trials of any sort, or fall into various temptations. Be assured and understand that the trial and proving of your faith bring out endurance and steadfastness and patience.

James 1:2–3 AMP

*When you choose courage over safety,
you will reap your own unique reward.*

*With God watching over you, you never
have to be afraid to face danger.*

Sometimes there's nothing wrong with playing it safe, considering your options, not rushing to follow the herd. Sometimes playing it safe can save you from financial ruin or physical harm. But the times you don't want to seek safety are the times when God is calling you to something good and noble, and that sometimes requires the proverbial leap of faith. If you hold back instead of leaping, you'll miss a great adventure. God doesn't want you to play it safe in the area of moral issues. He expects all His men to take a stand for what is right, to speak out whenever and wherever they see wrong being done. Stay courageous, my husband, and God will reward you appropriately, both in this life and in the next.

God grant me the courage not to give up what I think is right, even though I think it is hopeless.

Admiral Chester W. Nimitz

Be strong and let your heart take courage,
all you who wait for the LORD.

Psalm 31:24 NRSV

When you choose courage over safety,
you will reap your own unique reward.

Adversity is the weight training God
uses to strengthen you.

Your good character inspires both my
admiration and my trust.

The secret of success lies in realizing that lost opportunities and shut doors represent God's guidance.

Accept the things that don't go right in your life as signposts to turn you in a new and better direction.

A lost opportunity, a thwarted plan, a shut door— at first glance they all look like failure. But look more closely, and you'll see something else. Lost opportunities are simply opportunities with someone else's name on them. Thwarted plans are plans that weren't right for you. And a shut door? Look carefully, and you'll probably see a sign on it that reads, "Not your address. Try another door." Don't get discouraged when things don't go according to plan, when you get to what seemed to be an open door only to find it closed on you. This is simply God's way of steering you to the right path for you. Change your plan. Look for a new door. I have confidence that you'll always find your way.

I am satisfied that when the Almighty wants me to do or not do any particular thing he finds a way of letting me know.

Abraham Lincoln

The steps of the godly are directed by the LORD.
He delights in every detail of their lives.
Psalm 37:23 NLT

Forgiveness is the quickest way to propel yourself forward in life.

Don't waste your time stewing over things in the past that you can't change. Instead, move forward and focus on the future.

Unforgivingness holds you back. It's hard to reach out to new people when you're clinging to a grudge. It's hard to focus your energy on new ideas when you're staring at old hurts. And it's really hard to get a clear vision of the future if you're looking back at the past. The only way to move forward effectively is to leave grudges, hurts, and the past behind. Letting go of old grievances makes you lighter, makes it easier to run farther faster. When you forgive the people who hurt you, you drop that anger-drag and find yourself with something much more useful: a clean emotional engine, fueled with enthusiasm to move on with your life. When you let go of bitterness you can really go places.

> When you forgive, you in no way change the past— but you sure do change the future.
>
> Bernard Meltzer

Get along with each other, and forgive each other. If someone does wrong to you, forgive that person because the Lord forgave you.

Colossians 3:13 NCV

God will be with you in any adventure to which He calls you.

Always remember that God is with you no matter what.

Life is a series of adventures, isn't it? And sometimes a new adventure can look scary, even to a man as brave as you are. Illness, loss, risk— who knows what lies further down the road for us? Who knows what difficult decisions you will be called to make? One thing you can know: God will be with you every step of the way. That's why He wants you to keep your hero's attitude, to be ready to follow Him wherever He leads you. He wants you to be like the ancient hero Joshua, who refused to let giants scare him away from the Promised Land. I know God has your own Promised Land waiting for you. He'll make sure you get there.

> All the resources of the Godhead are at our disposal!
>
> Jonathan Goforth

Don't be afraid, for I am with you. Do not be dismayed, for I am your God. I will strengthen you. I will help you. I will uphold you with my victorious right hand.

Isaiah 41:10 NLT

One reason God gave you two arms
is so you can comfort your wife.

Your tenderness helps me
find new strength.

I appreciate the fact that you use your eyes to see when something's bothering me, and you use your ears to listen to my troubles. What I like best about you is when you use your strong arms to comfort me. I need that comfort when I'm discouraged or disheartened, when I'm hurt and need to be reminded that someone cares and that it will be all right. Life can throw some unexpected punches. Sometimes it can deliver a real emotional knockout. But knowing you're here with me and there for me, that you care about me, helps heal the hurts. Your arms around me remind me that God put us together, not only to share good times, but also to comfort each other in hard times.

In misery it is great comfort to have a companion.

John Lyly

Praise be to the God and Father of our Lord Jesus Christ. God is the Father who is full of mercy and comfort. He comforts us every time we have trouble, so when others have troubles we can comfort them with the same comfort God gives us.

2 Corinthians 1:3–4 NCV

A good dose of Bible reading is your best cure for doubt.

When you make your Bible your number one read, you make your soul healthy.

Doubt is a common affliction. Its symptoms vary, but the most common ones are fear, worry, a reluctance to move forward, and confusion. Doubt can make a man question his choices and fail to use his talents. It can blind him to the bright presence of God in the middle of sorrow or difficulty. But there is a powerful cure for doubt, and I hope you'll always reach for this cure when even the smallest symptoms of doubt arise. The cure is your Bible. In its pages you'll find megadoses of courage, hope, insight, and guidance, and evidence of love far beyond what even I, your wife, can ever give you. I hope you'll dose yourself often, because if you do we'll both benefit.

No spiritual discipline is more important than the intake of God's word.

Donald S. Whitney

Your word is a lamp to my feet and a light to my path.

Psalm 119:105 NKJV

The key to a good life is to be honest, especially with yourself.

When you are honest first with yourself, you'll find it easier to be honest with God and others.

Honesty is the best policy. We've heard that often enough, haven't we? And haven't we found it to be true! You avoid so many awkward social situations and misunderstandings simply by being honest. Honesty earns the respect and trust of others and keeps your moral compass set to heaven. Still, sometimes it is hard to be honest, especially with yourself. It's not always easy to admit your shortcomings and needs or to look at your true motivation for certain behavior. I know, because I often have a hard time being honest with myself. But honesty is the only tool for digging to the root of a problem. Honesty is the only broom that sweeps our hearts clean. Let's ask God to keep us honest always, with each other and with ourselves.

> Our lives improve only when we take chances—and the first and most difficult chance we can take is to be honest with ourselves.
>
> Walter Anderson

Search me, oh God, and know my heart;
test me and know my thoughts.

Psalm 139:23 NRSV

I will always think you're the best, with or without your hair.

Nothing time can do will erode my love for you.

You had me before hello. The first time I saw you, I knew you were one of a kind. You proved me right. Your smile could make my heart hit overdrive, and your kiss could curl my toes. I could happily give up beauty sleep to stay up talking with you. And you know what? You still have that effect on me. I love your sense of humor. I love the way I fit so well in your arms. I love your heart. I love your charming ways. I love the way you look at me with a gleam and a smile. I'll always look into your eyes and see a beautiful soul; who cares how many laugh lines sneak in around them? No matter how your body changes over the years, you'll always be my ideal man.

> True love's the gift which God has given to man alone beneath the heavens.
>
> Walter Scott

Listen! My lover! Look! Here he comes, leaping across the mountains, bounding over the hills.

Song of Solomon 2:8 NIV

Forgiveness is the quickest way to propel yourself forward in life.

The key to a good life is to be honest, especially with yourself.

God will be with you in any adventure to which He calls you.

Successful marriage is always a triangle, a man, a woman, and God.

Cecil Meyers

Without the help of the LORD it is useless to build
a home or guard a city.

Psalm 127:1 CEV